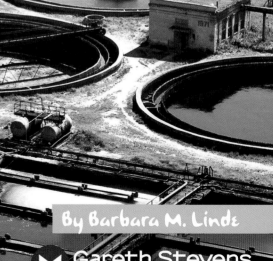

Where's the water?

WHAT IS WASTEWATER?

By Barbara M. Linde

Gareth Stevens
PUBLISHING

Please visit our website, www.garethstevens.com. For a free color catalog of all our high-quality books, call toll free 1-800-542-2595 or fax 1-877-542-2596.

Cataloging-in-Publication Data

Names: Linde, Barbara M.
Title: What is wastewater? / Barbara M. Linde.
Description: New York : Gareth Stevens Publishing, 2017. | Series: Where's the water? | Includes index.
Identifiers: ISBN 9781482446968 (pbk.) | ISBN 9781482446999 (library bound) | ISBN 9781482446975 (6 pack)
Subjects: LCSH: Water–Purification–Biological treatment. | Sewage–Purification–Biological treatment.
Classification: LCC TD475.L56 2017 | DDC 363.72'84–dc23

First Edition

Published in 2017 by
Gareth Stevens Publishing
111 East 14th Street, Suite 349
New York, NY 10003

Designer: Katelyn E. Reynolds
Editor: Kristen Nelson

Acknowledgements: Many thanks to Michael A. L. Roy for his insights and for the information about Sadhana Forest.

Photo credits: Cover, pp. 1, 11 Kekyalyaynen/Shutterstock.com; cover, pp. 1–24 (background) vitalez/Shutterstock.com; pp. 4–21 (circle splash) StudioSmart/Shutterstock.com; p. 5 wavebreakmedia/Shutterstock.com; p. 7 Sergey Dvornikov/Shutterstock.com; p. 9 AuntSpray/Shutterstock.com; p. 13 Lesterman/Shutterstock.com; p. 15 James P. Blair/National Geographic/Getty Images; p. 17 SSPL/Getty Images; p. 19 margouillat photo/Shutterstock.com; p. 20 Photofusion/Universal Images Group via Getty Images.

Printed in the United States of America

CPSIA compliance information: Batch #CS16GS : For further information contact Gareth Stevens, New York, New York at 1-800-542-2595.

CONTENTS

Words in the glossary appear in **bold** type
the first time they are used in the text.

DOWN THE DRAIN

Each person in the United States uses between 80 and 100 gallons (303 and 379 L) of water every day. Much of that is from flushing the toilet and taking baths and showers. The water used to wash clothes and dishes and do things like watering the garden can also add up fast.

What happens to water when you flush the toilet or let water run down the **drain**? You'll learn the answers to these questions as you read all about wastewater.

You might use as much as 36,500 gallons (138,168 L) of water a year!

5

WASTEWATER

Wastewater is water that has been used. It might have gone down a drain in your home. If you wash your car outside, the leftover soapy, dirty water runs down the street and into the drain. Businesses like factories sometimes dump their wastewater into lakes or rivers, even though it may have harmful **chemicals** in it.

Rain and melting snow create wastewater, too. That's because as **precipitation** flows over land, it may carry dirt, trash, oil from cars, and even **fertilizer** from farms.

Facts on Tap

The wastewater created by rain, snow, and other water that moves over land into nearby bodies of water is called runoff.

Wastewater can be harmful to the **environment**.

7

HOW DOES A
PUBLIC WATER SYSTEM WORK?

A lot of wastewater started as clean water! When you turn on the tap of a sink, you get clean, drinkable water. Underground pipes bring this water into your neighborhood. These pipes connect with smaller pipes that bring the water into your house.

When water goes down the drain or the toilets at your house, it runs into small wastewater pipes. Outside your house, these join with larger underground pipes called sewer mains. These join other larger pipes and carry waste to a wastewater treatment plant.

facts on Tap

People who live on a farm or far outside a city might get their water from a well on their land or have pipes connected to a well shared with neighbors.

If you live in a city or town, your house is probably part of the public water system.

LIQUID WASTE

A wastewater treatment plant purifies, or cleans, wastewater. Here's what commonly happens to liquid waste:

- Wastewater flows through screens to catch large matter. The water then flows into large tanks.

- Chemicals are added, making smaller waste **particles** clump together and heavy ones sink.

- The water is forced through sand, rocks, or man-made **filters**. Small, harmful particles stay behind. The water then flows into another tank.

- The chemical chlorine, **ultraviolet light**, or helpful bacteria and other bugs are used to kill anything harmful that's left.

Facts on Tap

The United States and Canada together use over 1 million miles (1.6 million km) of water pipeline to get water to their citizens. That's enough to circle Earth 40 times!

A water treatment plant never closes. It works all day, every day, to clean a community's water.

11

SOLID WASTE

Here's what happens to solid human waste, or biosolids, at a wastewater treatment plant:

- Biosolids sink to the bottom of the wastewater tanks. They're pumped into a machine that spins them around. This separates biosolids from grit, like sand and small rocks.

- The grit is cleaned and sent to a **landfill**. The biosolids are pumped into another tank.

- The biosolids are mixed with air, bacteria, and other tiny bugs, which eat most of the harmful particles.

- Biosolids may be used or sent to a landfill.

Facts on Tap

Your drinking water is purified and tested at a water treatment plant before it's sent through pipes to your house. Chemicals might be added to make it safer for you to drink.

There are many laws that set standards for wastewater. Biosolids must be tested, too, to be sure they meet these standards before they're used. They may become fertilizer!

CUYAHOGA: A RIVER ON FIRE

Wastewater can cause big problems if we're not careful. For many years, factories and homes dumped their waste right into the Cuyahoga River near Cleveland, Ohio. The river became full of trash and **sewage**. Nothing could live in it. It caught on fire at least 13 times, including on June 22, 1969.

This fire scared people already worried about harming the environment. In 1970, the National Environmental Protection Act (NEPA) went into effect. It created the Environmental Protection Agency (EPA).

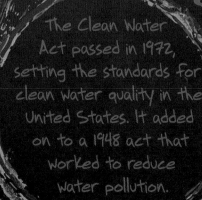

Facts on Tap

The Clean Water Act passed in 1972, setting the standards for clean water quality in the United States. It added on to a 1948 act that worked to reduce water pollution.

For many years, the Cuyahoga River, shown here, was badly polluted.

WATER ON THE
INTERNATIONAL SPACE STATION

Astronauts on the International Space Station (ISS) can't waste a drop of water! They can't flush the toilet or empty a drain into outer space. So how do they get clean water? And what do they do with wastewater?

The ISS uses a special water system that was made just for the station. All the water gets recycled—even **urine** and wastewater from showers! The system cleans so well that the astronauts can drink the recycled water.

Facts on Tap

NASA figured out a way to kill harmful bacteria in water. Companies here on Earth now use it to keep the water in swimming pools and drinking fountains safe and clean.

Astronaut Koichi Wakata has said, "Here on board the ISS, we turn yesterday's coffee into tomorrow's coffee."

17

WHAT'S YOUR WATER FOOTPRINT?

Your water footprint is the amount of water you use. That includes your wastewater and the water used to produce everything you buy or eat. When you know what your footprint is, you can figure out ways to lower it!

Reducing your water footprint is important because there's only a set amount of water on Earth. Some places on Earth already don't have enough water. Since water is needed for all life on Earth, we must take care not to waste it!

Facts on Tap

Some places don't have clean drinking water because they don't have any way to clean wastewater. **Conservation** groups often work in these places to make clean water more available.

The water footprint for this meal includes feeding the cow, growing the crops, making the food—and the plate—and shipping everything to the store. It also includes your car's gas to get to and from the restaurant!

19

WASTEWATER USE AT SADHANA FOREST

Sadhana Forest is a tree-planting and conservation project in southern India. The people there try to waste as little water as possible!

Those who live at Sadhana Forest pump their own water from underground by hand. They take showers with just a bucket of water and use only a little water to wash their hands. Dishwater is used to water their banana and papaya trees. The people use **composting** toilets that don't need to be flushed! Would you be able to live with so little water?

Shut this lid after use

The liquid from a composting toilet is stored in a tank. It's slowly let out into wetlands where plants take it in and clean it naturally. The solid waste is mixed with sawdust and left to sit for about a year. Then it's used as fertilizer.

Washing hands and face:
1 gallon (3.8 L)

running the dishwasher:
6 to 16 gallons (22.7 to 60.6 L)

brushing teeth:
less than 1 gallon (3.8 L)

flushing the toilet:
1 to 4 gallons (3.8 to 15 L)

Do You Waste Water?

With a little extra thought, you can reduce your water footprint and the amount of wastewater you produce!

running the washing machine:
25 to 40 gallons
(94.6 to 151.4 L)

watering the lawn
for 30 minutes:
60 gallons (227 L)

Filling a bathtub:
36 gallons (136.3 L)

taking a 15-minute shower:
75 gallons (284 L)

This information is from the United States Geological Survey.

GLOSSARY

chemical: matter that can be mixed with other matter to cause changes

composting: able to turn waste into matter that can be added to soil to make it better for growing things.

conservation: the care of the natural world

drain: the hole and pipe through which water or other liquid is carried out of a sink, tub, or off a street

environment: the natural world

fertilizer: something that makes soil better for growing crops and other plants

filter: something that collects bits from a liquid passing through

landfill: a place where waste is collected

particle: a very small piece of something

precipitation: rain, snow, sleet, or hail

sewage: waste matter from buildings that is carried away through sewers

ultraviolet light: a range of wavelengths in light beyond the violet end of the visible color sequence

urine: a yellow liquid containing water and waste products that flows out of an animal's body

FOR MORE INFORMATION

Books

Duke, Shirley Smith. *The Water Cycle*. New York, NY: AV2 by Weigl, 2017.

Yomtov, Nel. *Water/Wastewater Engineer*. Ann Arbor, MI: Cherry Lake Publishing, 2015.

Websites

How Urine Is Turned into Clean Water on Space Station
space.com/25171-how-urine-is-turned-into-clean-water-on-space-station-video.html
Take a virtual visit to the International Space Station. Listen to astronaut Koichi Wakata explain how the astronauts' wastewater is processed and recycled.

Sadhana Forest
sadhanaforest.org
Read more about the ways Sadhana Forest uses water and wastewater.

Wastewater Treatment for Youngsters
metrocouncil.org/Wastewater-Water/Publications-And-Resources/ES_kids_book-pdf.aspx
Find out how the twin cities of Minneapolis and St. Paul, Minnesota, treat wastewater.

INDEX